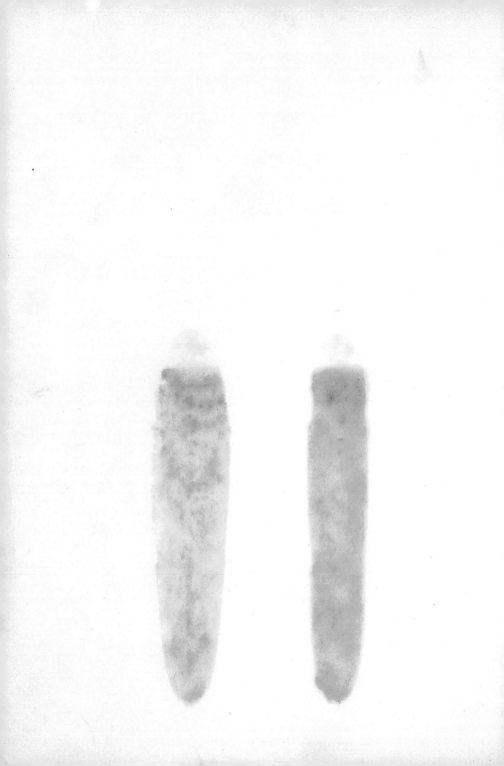

Dedicated to
TOMMY PULLMAN
and
Stripes, Grey Cat, Kitty Kaboodle, and Klondike
Jennie and Tessa
Birgitte and Sophie
Sophie and Potter
Neffie, Cassie, Gabie, Mouse, Muzzer, and T. S. Alleycat
and
Sandro
with love and thanks.

CLEO CATRA'S RIDDLE ? BOOK

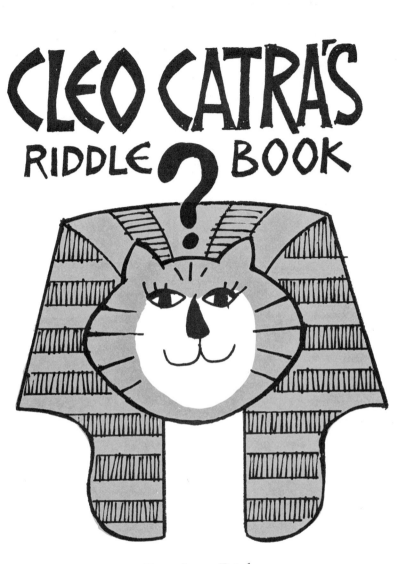

By *Ann Bishop*
Pictures by *Jerry Warshaw*

ELSEVIER/NELSON BOOKS
New York

Copyright © 1981 by Ann Bishop

Library of Congress Cataloging in Publication Data
Bishop, Ann.
    Cleo Catra's riddle book.

    SUMMARY: A book of riddles centering around Cleo
Catra, a cat of ancient Egypt.
    1. Riddles—Juvenile literature. [1. Riddles]
I. Warshaw, Jerry. II. Title.
PN6371.5.B49   398'.6   80-17104
ISBN 0-525-66706-7

Published in the United States by Elsevier/Nelson Books, a division of Elsevier-Dutton Publishing Company, Inc., New York. Published simultaneously in Don Mills, Ontario, by Nelson/Canada.

Printed in the U.S.A.   First Edition

10   9   8   7   6   5   4   3   2   1

Flip the pages for a Flip Movie

Long ago and long ago,
   and longer ago than that,
      Egypt was ruled, so I've been told,
         by a beautiful yellow cat!

What was her name?

?

Cleo Catra, of course!

Why was Cleo Catra so popular?
Why did Cleo Catra say "NO" all the time?

She had purrsonality.
Because she was Queen of Denial.

What are the little rivers that run into
    the River Nile?
What did the Court Artist call his painting of
    Cleo Catra?

The Juveniles.
A pawtrait.

She had a handsome young king
to help her rule Egypt.

Why did the King say his name was Tut Tut?
How do you say "Tut Tut" in Egyptian?
Do black cats really bring bad luck?
What did King Tut Tut wear to bed?
Why was King Tut Tut foaming at the mouth?

Because he tuttered.
Tut Tut in Egyptian.
That's just supurrstition—unless you are a mouse.
Purr-jamas.
He had soap flakes instead of corn flakes for breakfast.

?

What held up the roof in Cleo Catra and
  Tut Tut's palace?
What was Cleo Catra and Tut Tut's
  favorite room?
How did Cleo Catra buy cat food?
How did she know that there was something
  wrong with the cat food?

Caterpillars.
The kit-chen.
At so much purr can.
She had inside information.

Why did Tut Tut walk around holding an
    ice cream cone with two sparrows sitting on it?
What did Tut Tut take for a headache?
Why did Cleo Catra put her kittens in the trash
    barrel?
What did she use when she took the kittens
    for a ride?

He wanted to chill two birds with one cone. ?
Aspurrin.
It said "Put litter here."
A kitty car.

Egypt has some unusual features

What's a camel?
Where did Cleo Catra park her camel?
What do you name a camel that has no humps?

A horse that was a group project.
In a Camelot.
Humpfree.

Was Cleo Catra impressed by the stones in the
  pyramids?
Why are a joke and a pyramid alike?

No—she took them for granite.
They both have a point.

What did Cleo Catra say
when she saw her statue?

It Sphinx!

The royal dancers entertained the court

What do you call a row of cats doing high kicks?
What did the chorus feline call themselves?

A chorus feline.
The Rockittes.

What was their show known as?
What did they dance to?
What great honor did they win?

A cat-er-act.
Mewsic.
The A-Cat-emy Award.

Egypt is also famous for something scary. . .

What did Tut Tut call his female parent?
What do you get when you cross an Egyptian
 mother and a stove?
How do you catch Egyptian flu?

Mummy.
A red-hot mummy.
From your mummy.

What do you call a very small mummy?
What kind of music do mummies like?
What do you call a conference of mummies?

A minimum.
Ragtime.
A wrap session.

What are mummies?
Why didn't the mummy answer the phone?
What do you get when you cross a vampire bat
   and an Egyptian mummy?

Egyptians who are pressed for time.
She was all tied up.
Either a flying band aid or a gift-wrapped bat.

What happens to a mummy who eats too many
  archeologists?
What do you call a person who has sat in a tomb
  for 2000 years?

It gets a mummy ache.
A dummy.

Ɔ

Cleo Catra and Tut Tut are not the only
famous cats in history. There are many
others . . . .

What evil Chinese cat sneezes all the time?
Who is the most famous cat in the west?
What beautiful cat wore glass slippers?
What Irish cat is always looking for a pot of gold?

Fu Cat Chooo!
Puss-in-Butte.
Cinderalleycat.
A Leprocat.

What great cat president freed the mice?
What cat drove the mice out of Ireland?
What cat was Emperor of France?

Abraham Linkit.
Saint Catrick.
Napoleon Bonapuss.

What was the name of the first Astrocat?
What do you call a cat who loves to play
the drums?

Cl

Which cat won the story-telling contest?
What was the charge against the Old Lady Cat
    Who Lived in the Shoe?

The Cat-o-nine-tales.
Kitty litter.

What kind of cat came over on the Mayflower?
What scary cat kept the Early Settlers awake?
What do you call a cat that robs McDonald's?

A Purritan.
Pok-a-haunt-puss.
A cat Burger-lar.

Meanwhile, back at the palace . . .

Why did Tut Tut go into the candy business?
Why did Cleo Catra sweep the palace floor?
What is a water cooler?

He wanted to make a mint.
She was a do-it-yourself kit.
A thirst-aid kit.

What did Cleo Catra hang up at Christmas?
Who brought Christmas presents to the palace?

Mouseltoe.
Sandy Claws.

Cleo

and another famous cat!

What cat wears a mask, a cape, and weighs
   500 pounds?
What does Supurr Cat say?
What did Supurr Cat want for his birthday?
Where does Supurr Cat sleep?

Supurr Cat!
Here Fido, here Fido!
A catnip moose.
Any place he wants to.

There were oriental cats in the palace

What do you get when you cross
   two Siamese cats?
What did the Siamese cat wear for a disguise?
Why do Siamese cats have X-ray vision?
What do you get when you cross an angora cat
   and a kangaroo?

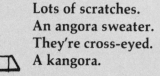

Lots of scratches.
An angora sweater.
They're cross-eyed.
A kangora.

and a few mice . . .

Why did Tut Tut eat cheese?
What time is it when twelve cats chase
   a mouse?
What do you call a mouse's coat?
What do you call very small mice?

So he could watch the mouse hole with
   baited breath.
Twelve after one.
Micky Mantle.
Minimize.

Cleo

and some other animals

What's long, skinny, and says hith hith?
What kind of dial should you stay away from?
What do you call a fat cat?

A snake with a lisp.
A crocodile.
A flabby tabby.

Who is the fattest cat in the River Nile?
Why did Cleo Catra put oil on her pet monkey?
What do you get if you cross a cat and
a hyena?

The hippo-pot-a-puss.
She wanted to see a monkeyshine.
A gigglepuss.

Cleo

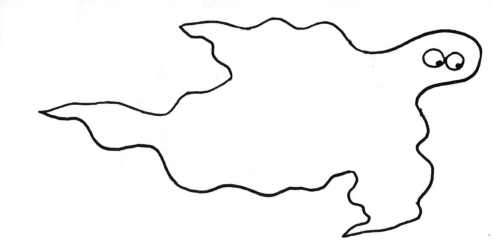

Where there are cats,
there is likely to be a witch

Why did the Egyptian witch live in the desert?
What did Cleo Catra say when the witch
   was afraid to swim in the Red Sea?
Why did the witch give out her phone number?
What did the witch say when the ghost
   visited her?
What city has the most witches?

She was a sand witch.
"Chicken sand witch!"
So people could dial a scare.
"Be my ghost!"
Witchita.

What was Cleo Catra when she rode on
  the witch's broom?
How do witches drink tea?
What do witches eat on picnics?

A witch hiker!
With cups and sorcerers.
Deviled eggs, deviled ham, and devil's food cake.

What's a witch's favorite fairy story?
Which witch has the best hearing?

Ghouldilocks.
The eeriest.

and so, as the sun sinks slowly into the river Nile, we say good-bye to Cleo Catra and Tut Tut . . . .

Will we hear from them again?

Purr-haps.